TRUSTING *the* UNSEEN

Unlocking the Power of Intuition

© 2025 S. Shelly

All rights reserved.

No part of this publication may be reproduced, stored in a retrieval system, or transmitted in any form or by any means — electronic, mechanical, photocopying, recording, or otherwise — without the prior written permission of the copyright holder, except in the case of brief quotations used in reviews or articles.

Published by Stardust Press
United Kingdom

ISBN: 978-1-9193876-1-1

Printed in the United Kingdom
First Edition

Table of Contents

Introduction — The Ancient Wisdom of Inner Knowing

Part One — Remembering Your Inner Voice

- What Intuition Really Is   8

- Why You Lost Touch With It   15

- How Intuition Speaks to You   22

Part Two — Creating Space for Intuition

- Creating Space to Hear Yourself Again   34

- What Gets in the Way of Intuition   43

- How Intuition Speaks — So You Can Recognise It   53

Part Three — Understanding Your Inner Language

- The Difference Between Intuition & Fear   64

- Strengthening Your Intuitive Confidence   80

- When Intuition Leads You Somewhere Unexpected   92

Part Four — Living From Inner Alignment

- Integrating Intuition Into Daily Life   103

- When Intuition Conflicts With Other People's Expectations   115

- Becoming the Version of You Who Trusts Yourself Fully   126

- Signs You're Living From Intuition   139

Final Part — The Evolution of You

- Closing Chapter — The Quiet Revolution Within You   153

Epilogue — The Light You Carry Forward

The Ancient Wisdom of Inner Knowing

"What is meant for you will never bypass you. But you must be quiet enough to hear the path as it calls your name."

Long before our lives became loud — before constant noise and expectations filled our minds, before the world taught us to mistrust ourselves — humans lived by intuition.

Not as a mystical ability.
Not as something rare or gifted.
But as a natural way of moving through life.

Ancient cultures, elders, healers, mystics, and everyday people trusted their inner knowing to guide their choices, their relationships, their survival, and their belonging.

Intuition wasn't rare.

It wasn't doubted.

It was respected.

It was understood as the quiet language of truth — a connection to the deeper intelligence that lives inside every human being.

People trusted:

- the sensation in the body

- the whisper in the heart

- the pull toward or away

- the instinctive yes

- the instinctive no

- the knowing without explanation

This wasn't superstition.

It was wisdom.

- Older than thought.

- Older than fear.

- Older than the world we live in now.

Intuition was our original navigation system.
And somewhere along the way — we forgot.

🌱 Why We Lost What Was Once Natural

As society grew louder, expectations multiplied.

- Logic was placed above all else.
- Information replaced reflection.
- Performance overshadowed presence.

And slowly, quietly, we drifted from our inner knowing.

We learned to mistrust the sensations in our bodies.

- To dismiss the whisper in our hearts.

- To ignore the quiet internal "no."

- To argue with the gentle internal "yes."

- We traded instinct for intellect.
- Wisdom for noise.
- Truth for approval.
- Alignment for expectation.

We didn't lose intuition.

We just stopped hearing it.

🌿 The Return to Intuition Is a Return to Ourselves

This book isn't teaching you something new.

It's guiding you back to something ancient.

- something your ancestors trusted

- something your body remembers

- something your soul recognizes instantly

You're not learning intuition — you're remembering it.

The original language, your inner wisdom has always spoken.

A wisdom older than logic.

Older than fear.
Older than the noise around you.

🌿 Why This Matters Now

Modern life is loud — louder than any time before us.

- Information is constant.
- Comparison is constant.
- Noise is constant.
- Expectation is constant.

But the ancient wisdom hasn't disappeared.
It's only been drowned out.

This book is your pathway back to that quiet knowing — not to retreat from life, but to meet it with clarity, alignment, and inner authority.

Intuition is not the enemy of logic.
It is the foundation of wisdom.

It allows you to move through the world

- not blindly,
- not reactively,
- not anxiously

but connected to the deeper guidance
humans have trusted for thousands of years.

This book is not about creating a new you.

It's about remembering the truest you — the one who already knows the way.

What Intuition Really Is

Intuition is one of the most misunderstood abilities we have as human beings.

People often imagine it as something mystical, unexplainable, reserved only for the deeply spiritual or the unusually gifted.

But intuition is not rare.

It is not dramatic.

It is not strange.

Intuition is natural.

Instinctive.

Built into you.

It is the quiet inner intelligence you were born with.

Before the world shaped your mind, before life conditioned your reactions, before fear became louder than truth — your intuition was the voice you trusted most.

You can see this clearly in children.

- They express what they feel without hesitation.

- They pull away from what doesn't feel right.

- They light up when something resonates.

- They move toward joy with ease.

- They sense the energy of a room instantly.

- They trust their instinct because they haven't yet learned not to.

As adults, we become masters of logic — but beginners in listening to ourselves.

Intuition is still inside you, but it often sits beneath layers of:

- Overthinking

- Worry

- external pressure

- emotional wounds

- expectations

- conditioning

- self-doubt

Yet through all of this noise, your intuition never disappears.

It simply waits for you to remember it.

So what is intuition?

It is the part of you that knows without needing to analyse.

It is:

- a quiet inner clarity

- a sensation in your chest

- a whisper in your mind

- a soft nudge

- a feeling that something is right or wrong

- a knowing that arrives quickly and calmly

It does not come with panic.

It does not come with arguments.

It does not come with pressure.

Intuition is steady.

Neutral.

Clear.

When you feel intuition, you feel truth — not the mind's version of truth, but your body's truth.

Intuition speaks differently than fear.

Fear is loud.
Intuition is quiet.

Fear demands.
Intuition guides.

Fear creates chaos.
Intuition brings peace.

Fear pushes.
Intuition gently pulls.

This chapter is your first step in recognising the difference.

Because once you understand what intuition truly is, you'll begin to see it everywhere —

- in your thoughts,

- in your emotions,

- in your body,

- in the way life unfolds around you.

Your intuition has never stopped speaking — You just stopped identifying its voice.

Together, we will change that.

By the end of this journey, you will not only understand intuition —

- you will trust it,

- listen to it,

- and live by it.

This isn't about becoming "more spiritual."

It's about becoming more you.

Why You Lost Touch With It

You were born intuitive.

You arrived into this world with a natural ability to feel truth, sense energy, read people, and recognise what was right or wrong for you — long before you had words to express it.

Every single human starts life this way.

So why do so many adults feel disconnected from their intuition?

Why do people say,

- "I don't trust myself,"
- "I don't know what I feel,"

Or

- "I'm confused about what's right for me"?

The answer is simple:

Life slowly teaches you to stop listening.

Not because you did anything wrong, but because the world around you trained your mind to speak louder than your inner voice.

🌿 How it begins

As children, we sense things naturally.

- We react instantly.
- We trust our feelings.
- We choose without hesitation.

But as you grow, you begin to absorb the beliefs and behaviours around you.

You're taught to:

- be "reasonable"
- follow rules
- be polite even when it feels wrong

- put others' feelings first
- ignore discomfort
- explain everything logically
- fear mistakes
- seek approval
- hide emotions

And slowly but surely, you shift from: "feeling first" to "thinking first".

Your natural instincts become buried under layers of learned behaviour.

The world rewards logic — not intuition

Society praises:

- being rational
- being practical
- being predictable
- being "sensible"

Feelings, sensitivity, inner knowing, gut instincts — these are often dismissed or labelled as:

- overreacting
- being too emotional
- being dramatic
- being irrational

So you learn to suppress them.

To question them.

To apologise for them.

Eventually, you stop recognising intuition altogether — not because it disappeared, but because it became drowned out.

Life experiences shape your trust in yourself.

Heartbreak, rejection, criticism, betrayal, disappointment — these moments leave emotional fingerprints.

You may have learned to:

- doubt yourself
- second-guess your feelings
- mistrust your judgement
- ignore your body's signals
- avoid taking risks
- silence your instincts
- choose logic over emotion

Every time your inner voice was ignored, dismissed, or punished, you subconsciously learned that intuition wasn't safe.

But none of this means you lost your intuition.
It simply means you stopped hearing it clearly.

 And then... something happens

One day, the way you've been living stops working.

You start feeling:

- overwhelmed
- drained
- out of alignment
- unsure
- disconnected from yourself

You feel a pull to slow down, re-evaluate, rethink, reconnect.

This moment — this discomfort — is often your intuition's first attempt to return to the surface.

It speaks through:

- restlessness
- body tension
- emotional exhaustion
- dissatisfaction
- the sense that "something feels off"
- the quiet thought that whispers, "There must be more than this."

This chapter is your reminder that nothing is wrong with you.

- You haven't failed.

- You didn't "lose your abilities."

You simply adapted to a world that taught you to silence them.

But now…

you are learning to listen again.

And intuition — like any natural ability — becomes strong the moment you pay attention to it.

- You haven't lost your inner voice.
- You've just been living too loudly to hear it.

And all of that changes now.

How Intuition Speaks to You

Intuition isn't something you need to hunt for.

It's not hiding.

It's not waiting for you to meditate for an hour or reach some mystical state.

Your intuition has been speaking to you every single day — through your body, your energy, your emotions, and the quiet thoughts that appear without effort.

The real question isn't:

"Do I have intuition?" but
"Do I notice how it speaks to me?"

Once you learn the language of your intuition, you'll realise it has been guiding you all along.

🌿 1. Intuition Speaks Through Your Body

Your body is the first place intuition shows up.

- It reacts faster than your mind.

- It senses truth before you can explain it.

- It feels energy before you can articulate it.

When something is right for you:

- your chest feels open

- your breath deepens

- your shoulders relax

- your stomach feels calm

- your energy expands

- you feel grounded and steady

- you sense "yes" before thinking "yes"

When something is wrong for you:

- your stomach tightens
- your throat feels restricted
- your breath becomes shallow
- your body feels heavy
- your energy contracts
- your heart feels unsettled
- you sense "no" even before you know why

Your body always knows.

It reacts instantly, honestly, and without overthinking.

🌿 2. Intuition Speaks Through Your Emotions

Your emotions are messengers.

- Not problems.
- Not weaknesses.
- Not inconveniences.

They reveal:

- what matters to you

- what drains you

- what inspires you

- what scares you

- what you desire

- what you're done with

- what feels aligned and what doesn't

If something makes you feel:

- peaceful

- excited

- comforted

- uplifted

- inspired

...that's intuition signalling yes.

If something makes you feel:

- uneasy
- irritated
- tense
- saddened

- anxious
- drained

…that's intuition signalling no.

Emotions are not random.

They're intuitive signals in disguise.

🌿 3. Intuition Speaks Through Your Energy

This is the part most people ignore —yet it's one of the clearest signals you'll ever receive.

Pay attention to:

- what drains you
- what lifts you
- who exhausts you

- who energises you
- what situations feel heavy
- what environments feel light
- where your spirit feels calm
- where it feels suffocated

Your energy never lies.

If something feels heavy, forced, or sticky — there's a reason.

If something feels expansive, warm, or peaceful — there's a reason.

You don't need to justify it.

You just need to notice it.

🌿 4. Intuition Speaks Through Sudden Clarity

This is the quiet knowing that appears out of

nowhere.

Moments like:

- "I don't know why, but this doesn't feel right."

- "I just know I need to do this."

- "I can sense something is off."

- "I feel like I shouldn't go."

- "I need to reach out to this person."

- "I suddenly understand what I need to do."

Intuitive clarity is quick.

Light.

Effortless.

It arrives without needing analysis, and it often feels like a thought simply placed into your mind.

This is intuition at its purest.

🌿 5. Intuition Speaks Through Timing

You know those moments where everything just… lines up?

You leave the house one minute later and avoid something.

You delay something and it turns out to be perfect timing.

You think of someone just before they call.

You walk somewhere "randomly" and meet the exact person you needed.

This is intuition guiding your timing.

We won't go deep into synchronicity yet but for now, recognise this:

"Intuition is not only what you feel — it's when you feel it"

Sometimes the timing itself is the message.

🌱 6. Intuition Speaks in Silence

When everything else is quiet — when you pause, breathe, slow down —intuition rises like something floating to the surface.

This is why:

- long showers bring clarity

- quiet walks reveal answers

- sitting alone brings truth

- driving without music sparks ideas

- early mornings feel intuitive

- late-night thoughts feel honest

Silence is intuition's favourite language.

When you stop forcing answers, they arrive naturally.

🌿 **Your intuition is already speaking — now you are learning how to listen.**

As you move through this book, you'll begin noticing:

- signals you used to ignore

- patterns you didn't see before

- clarity that was always there

- guidance hidden in everyday moments

Intuition is not a skill you learn — it's a voice you remember.

And now that you're learning its language, you're ready for the next part:

Strengthening it.

Creating Space to Hear Yourself Again

Your intuition isn't quiet.

Your life is loud.

Most people don't struggle with intuition because they "don't have it."

They struggle because they're surrounded by noise — external noise, mental noise, emotional noise, digital noise — and intuition cannot rise above it.

Intuition is a whisper.

Overthinking is a shout.

And modern life is an endless crowd.

To reconnect with your intuition, you don't need to escape the world, move to a cabin in the forest, or sit in meditation for hours a day.

You simply need small pockets of space where your inner voice can breathe.

Why silence matters

Your mind is loud.
Your intuition is subtle.

Your mind speaks in sentences.
Intuition speaks in sensations.

Your mind reacts quickly.
Intuition responds clearly.

If your mind is constantly multitasking, rushing, analysing, or anticipating, your intuition won't get a chance to be heard.

Stillness doesn't create intuition — it reveals it.

🌿 The Power of a Pause

Most intuitive breakthroughs happen in small moments:

- a deep breath

- a slow exhale

- a pause before replying

- a moment of stillness before choosing

- a quiet second where your emotions catch up

It doesn't take long.

Sometimes a three-second pause is all it takes to feel the truth.

In that pause, your nervous system resets.

- Your mind softens.

- Your body speaks.

Try it the next time you're unsure about something. Before acting, ask yourself:

"How does this feel in my body?"

The first sensation is intuition.

🌱 Micro-Moments of Stillness

You don't need to overhaul your entire life to reconnect with your intuition.

Tiny adjustments are enough.

Here are simple practices that open the door:

1. Quiet coffee or tea

- No phone.

- No noise.

    - Just breathe.
    - Feel your body.
    - Connect inward.

2. A few minutes of stillness each morning

    - Sit.
    - Hands on your lap.
    - Breathe.
    - No expectations.

3. Walk without headphones

    - Let your thoughts settle.
    - Notice sensations.
    - Let clarity rise.

4. Take small "mind breaks" during the day

    - Look out of the window.
    - Stretch.
    - Exhale.
    - Reset.

5. End the day without screens

    - Let your nervous system unwind.
    - Let your energy settle.

None of these require effort — just intention.

🌿 Your inner voice lives in the spaces you create

Most people think intuition requires:

- meditation

- rituals

- deep spiritual practices

But really, it requires:

- quiet

- presence

- awareness

- breathing

- softness

When you create space, intuition moves toward you.

When you rush, intuition steps back.

When you slow down, clarity arrives.

When you listen, intuition shows itself.

Your inner guidance has been waiting for this — a quiet moment to be heard again.

🌿 **You don't need to find intuition — You just need to make room for it.**

Your intuition is not distant, hidden, or complicated.

- It's close.
- It's present.
- It's patient.

You reconnect simply by giving yourself the space to feel what you feel…

- without judgement
- without pressure
- without interruptions.

This chapter is your reminder that slowing down is not weakness.

Stillness is not laziness.

Quiet is not unproductive.

Silence is where your truth comes home.

And now that space has been created…

your intuition is ready to rise.

What Gets In the Way of Intuition

Your intuition is never gone.

It's never broken.

It never stops trying to guide you.

But guidance can be hard to hear when there's interference.

Most people don't lack intuition — they're just carrying too much noise, too much urgency, too much pressure to hear themselves clearly.

Intuition is quiet clarity.

Everything that blocks it is loud.

Let's look at the most common things that stand between you and your inner wisdom — and how to gently move them aside.

🌿 1. Overthinking: The Mind Taking the Steering Wheel

Overthinking isn't a flaw.

It's a protection strategy.

Your mind thinks it's keeping you safe by predicting every possibility, analysing every angle, controlling every outcome.

But intuition doesn't speak the language of logic.

It speaks the language of knowing.

When your mind is trying to solve, intuition can't get a word in.

You don't need to stop thinking — you just need to soften it.

- A slower breath.

- A longer pause.

- A moment to shift from thinking about your life to listening within it.

🌿 2. Self-Doubt: The Voice That Questions Every Yes

Self-doubt is loud.

Intuition is immediate.

You feel a truth — and then doubt arrives to dismantle it.

- "What if I'm wrong?"
- "What if I'm being dramatic?"
- "What if I mess this up?"
- "What if this feeling isn't real?"

Self-doubt is the echo of old conditioning, not your present truth.

Intuition is the first response.

Doubt is the second.

Trust the first.

🌿 3. Old Patterns: Stories You Outgrew But Still Carry

Your intuition belongs to who you are now.

Your patterns belong to who you were then.

Sometimes you're not hearing your intuition — you're hearing the past replaying itself.

The past tries to keep you small.

Intuition tries to help you expand.

Patterns say:
- "Play it safe."
- "Don't make a mistake."

- "Stay where you are."

Intuition says:

- "You've outgrown this."
- "This isn't aligned anymore."
- "It's time to evolve."

The moment you notice the difference, your power returns.

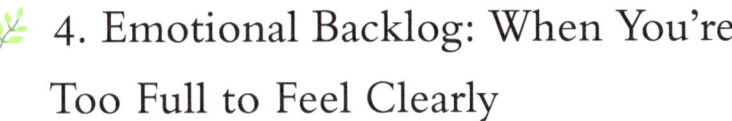 4. Emotional Backlog: When You're Too Full to Feel Clearly

Emotions don't disappear just because you move on.

They wait...

- They wait for quiet moments.
- They wait for safety.
- They wait until you slow down enough to feel them.

When you have an emotional backlog — unprocessed stress, grief, resentment, fear, fatigue — intuition gets muffled.

Not because it's weak, but because your heart is crowded.

Feelings need space to be acknowledged.

Intuition needs space to be heard.

When you release one, you uncover the other.

🌿 5. Urgency: When You're Moving Too Fast to Notice Truth

Urgency is the enemy of clarity.

Every intuitive misstep happens when you decide too quickly, respond out of pressure, or choose from a place of fear.

Intuition never rushes you.

Fear does.

If a decision feels frantic, it's not intuition — it's survival mode.

Slow down, even for a breath.

Truth can be felt in stillness that panic can't reach.

🌿 6. External Noise: Everyone Else's Opinions, Expectations, and Energy

Sometimes intuition is blocked not by your inner world but by everyone else's.

- What people think you should do.
- What they expect from you.
- How they react to your choices.
- What they fear for you.

- What they want from you.

When you're tuned into everyone else, you tune out yourself.

Intuition isn't found in agreement.
It's found in alignment.

Turn down the world so you can turn up yourself.

🌿 Clearing the Path Back to Yourself

You don't need to "fix" yourself to reconnect with your intuition.

You don't need to become more spiritual, more disciplined, more confident, or more certain.

You just need to remove what's blocking the signal.

When you:

- slow down

- soften your mind

- breathe deeper

- feel your body

- unpack old stories

- release urgency

and listen inward…

intuition rises naturally.

Because intuition isn't something you learn — it's something you remember.

🌿 **Your inner wisdom is already here**

Always has been.

Always will be.

It's buried under noise, not lost.

Covered, not gone.

Dimmed, not disappeared.

And every moment you choose stillness, honesty, presence, or courage…you clear another layer.

Part Five is your reminder:

Intuition doesn't hide from you.

It waits for you.

And the more you clear the path, the louder it becomes.

How Intuition Speaks – So You Can Recognise It

Intuition doesn't shout for your attention.

It doesn't argue, convince, or explain.

It speaks softly, simply, and immediately. But once you know its voice, you'll recognize it anywhere.

Most people don't ignore intuition — they just don't recognize its language.

This chapter teaches you the ways intuition communicates, so when it arrives, you know it's truth and not fear, not habit, not overthinking, not someone else's voice.

Intuition has many forms, but it never tries to confuse you.

It always speaks in clarity.

Let's explore the ways it speaks so you can finally hear it.

🌿 1. Intuition as a Sensation: The Body Speaks First

Your body feels truth before your mind understands it.

Intuition often shows up as:

- a softening
- an expansion
- a sense of ease
- a quiet "yes" in your chest
- a grounded calm
- a warm pull toward something
- a subtle recoil away from something

Your body reacts faster than your thoughts. It knows what's aligned before you can explain why.

If something feels heavy, tight, or contracted — your body is telling you no.

If something feels open, warm, or spacious — your body is telling you yes.

Intuition speaks through sensation because truth is physical long before it becomes logical.

🌿 2. Intuition as a Whisper: The First Honest Thought

Intuition is the first thought.

Fear is the second.

Overthinking is the third, fourth, and fifth.

That first quiet message — the one you often dismiss because it feels too simple — is the real one.

It's the thought that arrives before analysis, before doubt, before you start rehearsing outcomes.

It's quick.

Clear.

Uncomplicated.

Sometimes intuition is a single sentence, like:

- "This isn't right."
- "I don't trust this."
- "Reach out."
- "Go for it."
- "Not now."
- "This is the direction."

Your mind debates.

Intuition states.

🌿 3. Intuition as Resonance: The Feeling of Alignment

Some truths don't make sense — they just feel right.

You don't know how you know, you just do.

That feeling of resonance is intuition's language:

- a deep internal click,

- a sense of being pulled forward,

- a gentle certainty that doesn't need proof.

Resonance isn't loud or dramatic.

It's quiet confidence. It's alignment felt from the inside out.

4. Intuition as Discomfort: A Message Disguised as Tension

Not all intuitive messages feel good.

Some feel like:

- "Something is off."
- "I don't want to be here."
- "This doesn't fit anymore."
- "I'm shrinking around this person."

Discomfort isn't fear — it's information.

Intuition doesn't try to protect your feelings.
It tries to protect your truth.

Any time something feels "off," that's intuition asking you to pay attention.

🌿 5. Intuition as a Quiet Knowing: The Truth With No Reason

Sometimes you just know.

- No explanation.
- No evidence.
- No logic.

Just a calm certainty.

This is the purest form of intuition — truth without justification.

- It doesn't argue for itself.
- It doesn't need validation.
- It arrives fully formed.

The mind says, "Explain it."

Intuition says, "You already feel it."

🌿 6. Intuition as Clarity After Stillness

When you slow down, truth rises to the surface on its own.

- After a pause
- a breath
- a moment of silence
- a short walk
- a quiet night
- a calm morning

answers that were tangled become untangled.

What felt confusing becomes obvious.

What felt muddy becomes simple.

Clarity isn't created by force — it emerges when space is made.

Intuition often arrives right after you stop trying.

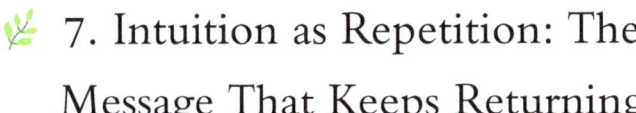 7. Intuition as Repetition: The Message That Keeps Returning

When intuition wants you to hear something, it repeats itself.

- The same thought.
- The same feeling.
- The same nudge.
- The same whisper.

Again and again.

It returns not to annoy you but because it's important.

You can ignore intuition, but it will keep circling back until you listen.

🌿 Learning Your Intuitive Language

You don't have to master all of these.

Just notice the ones that feel most familiar.

Everyone has a primary intuitive channel — a default way truth speaks to them.

For some, it's sensation.

For others, it's knowing.

For others, it's the whisper.

For others, it's resonance.

Your job isn't to force intuition to speak a certain way — it's to learn the way it already speaks to you.

🌿 Intuition Doesn't Try to Be Heard — It Just Is

When you quiet the noise, you realize intuition has been speaking all along.

- Not dramatically.
- Not with urgency.
- Not with pressure.

Just truth.
Soft, steady truth.

Part Six is your reminder:

intuition is always speaking — you're just learning the language.

And once you learn the language, you'll never again mistake fear for truth or noise for guidance.

Your inner voice becomes unmistakable.

The Difference Between Intuition & Fear

If you listen closely, your intuition will guide you back into the here and now — one moment, one breath, one choice at a time — because the fears your mind creates about the future are almost always unfounded, shadows of a tomorrow that may never exist.

Anxiety is often your mind trying to survive a future that hasn't happened.

It pulls you into imagined scenarios, global worries, and possibilities your heart has never lived — and may never live.

Intuition doesn't exist in those places.
It cannot guide you through futures that aren't real.

Intuition lives only in the present.

When you stay here — in this moment — you reconnect with clarity.

You become grounded in what you can influence.

You stop carrying the weight of situations that are not yours to control.

Most of the fears that overwhelm you are triggered by:

- News
- Uncertainty
- global events
- outcomes you cannot predict
- situations you cannot influence

Your subconscious reacts to them as if they are happening in your own life.

But intuition brings you back to what is happening — your breath, your steps, your choices, your day.

When you move one moment at a time, you discover that nearly every problem becomes manageable.

And many things you fear never become problems at all.

Your intuition doesn't ask you to solve the entire future.

It simply asks you to take the next right step — and trust that the rest will unfold when it's time.

If intuition is your inner compass, fear is the static that distorts the signal.

Most people don't struggle to feel their intuition — they struggle to separate it from the voice of fear.

Fear feels urgent.

Intuition feels certain.

Fear overwhelms.

Intuition whispers.

Fear demands.
Intuition guides.

And yet... the two can feel confusingly similar when you're in the middle of trying to choose, decide, or step forward.

This chapter is your clarity. A way to finally tell them apart so you stop mistaking warning for truth and truth for danger.

🌿 Intuition and Fear Speak From Different Places

Fear speaks from history.
Intuition speaks from presence.

Fear comes from your protective self.

Intuition comes from your deeper self.

Fear says, "This is risky."
Intuition says, "This is aligned."

One moves you forward.
The other holds you back.

Both try to protect you — but only one represents your truth.

🌿 1. **Fear is Loud.

Intuition is Quiet.**

Fear yells so you'll listen.

Intuition whispers because it trusts you.

Fear pushes.
Intuition nudges.

Fear uses pressure.
Intuition uses clarity.

If a feeling is shouting, panicking, or demanding immediacy — that's fear.

Intuition never rushes.
It simply states.

🌿 2. **Fear Contracts the Body.**

Intuition Expands It.**

Your body tells the truth even when your mind can't.

Fear often shows up as:

- Tightness
- Clenching
- Shrinking

- Closing
- frozen energy
- urgency in the chest
- tension in the gut

Intuition feels like:

- spaciousness

- warmth

- grounding

- openness

- a subtle forward pull

- a calm "yes" you can't explain

Fear restricts.

Intuition opens.

🌿 3. **Fear Asks "What If?"

Intuition Says "This Is."**

Fear imagines.

It creates scenarios, doubts, catastrophes, and possibilities.

It tries to protect you by showing you everything that could go wrong.

Intuition doesn't imagine.

It recognizes.
It tells the truth without needing reasons.
It offers direction without requiring a story.

Fear forecasts the future.
Intuition speaks from the present.

🌿 4. **Fear Needs Proof.

Intuition Needs Nothing.**

Fear wants:

- evidence
- reassurance
- explanations
- guarantees

It wants certainty before you move.

But intuition doesn't argue for itself.

It doesn't persuade or justify.

It simply lands.

- You feel it.

- You know it.

Even if you can't explain why.

🌱 5. **Fear Feels Like Panic. Intuition Feels Like Knowing.**

A simple distinction:

- Fear feels chaotic.

- Intuition feels clear.

Fear is noisy, fast, destabilizing, overwhelming.

Intuition is calm, steady, and grounded — even when it's telling you something difficult.

Yes, intuition can say "walk away."

Yes, intuition can say "this isn't right."

But it says it with clarity, not panic.

Fear shakes you.

Intuition settles you.

 6. **Fear Protects You.

Intuition Directs You.**

Fear keeps you safe.

Intuition keeps you aligned.

Fear wants to prevent harm.

Intuition wants to guide growth.

Fear keeps you where you are.

Intuition leads you where you're meant to go.

Fear holds on.

Intuition releases.

Fear hides.

Intuition reveals.

7. **Fear is Conditional.

Intuition is Consistent.**

Fear changes with your mood, stress level, and environment.

It appears stronger when you're tired, overwhelmed, or insecure.

Intuition doesn't fluctuate.
It stays the same even when you feel different.

If the feeling changes as your emotions change — it's fear.

If the message stays the same no matter how you feel — it's intuition.

🌿 How to Tell Them Apart in the Moment

The next time you're unsure, ask:

- Does this feel urgent or clear?

Urgent = fear.
Clear = intuition.

- Does this tighten my body or soften it?

Tight = fear.
Soft = intuition.

- Is this coming from past pain or present truth?

Past = fear.
Present = intuition.

- Do I feel panicked or guided?

Panicked = fear.
Guided = intuition.

- Does this feeling get louder the longer I ignore it?

Louder = fear.
Steady = intuition.

🌿 Fear Isn't the Enemy

— It's the Evidence You're Growing

You'll never "get rid" of fear — and you don't need to.

Fear simply means:

- You're expanding.
- You're breaking patterns.
- You're stepping into something new.
- You're moving toward truth.

The goal is not to stop fear but to stop confusing it with intuition.

🌿 When You Know the Difference, Everything Changes

- You stop holding yourself back because of old stories.

- You stop abandoning yourself because of imagined outcomes.

- You stop doubting your inner voice because you know how it speaks.

You stop mistaking protection for guidance.

And you start living from alignment — not avoidance.

This chapter is your reminder:

fear will always speak first,

but intuition will always speak truth.

When you know the difference, you stop living from old wounds and start living from inner wisdom.

Strengthening Your Intuitive Confidence

Intuition is a relationship.

And like any relationship, it deepens with trust.

You already have intuitive wisdom.

What you're learning now is how to believe it without overthinking, without searching for permission, and without abandoning yourself when doubt tries to return.

Intuitive confidence isn't built through perfection — it's built through small acts of self-trust that accumulate over time.

This chapter teaches you how to strengthen that trust until your inner voice feels like home.

🌱 1. Start Small, Not Big

People lose trust in their intuition because they try to test it only on life's biggest decisions:

- Should I quit?
- Should I stay?
- Should I end this?
- Should I move?

Those questions carry too much pressure for a beginning.

Confidence grows from the small things:

- What do I want to eat?
- Who do I want to see?
- Do I want to say yes or no?
- Does this feel energizing or draining?
- Do I need rest or movement right now?

Every small intuitive decision whispers to your nervous system:

"I can trust myself."

And that whisper becomes a foundation.

🌿 2. Act Before Doubt Arrives

Intuition speaks first.

Doubt arrives quickly.

The longer you wait, the louder fear becomes.

Confidence grows when you shorten the distance between intuitive knowing and intuitive action.

It can be as tiny as:

- sending the message
- taking the walk

- saying no
- saying yes
- pausing
- stepping back
- putting your hand on your heart and breathing

Act quickly on the small nudges, and intuition becomes easier to hear — because it knows you're listening.

🌿 3. Keep an "Intuition Wins" List

Your mind remembers your mistakes.

It doesn't automatically remember your intuitive victories.

But you have so many — times when something felt off, or felt right, or felt important without any logical reason…

...and you were right.

Start keeping track.

- Write down moments when following your intuition helped you.

- Write down the moments when ignoring it didn't.

With time, the pattern becomes undeniable:

You can trust your inner voice.

You always could.

4. Let Intuition Be Simple

Intuition isn't dramatic.

It doesn't arrive with trumpets or lightning.

It arrives with quiet clarity.

- A soft nudge.
- A simple truth.

Confidence grows when you stop expecting intuition to feel magical or extraordinary.

It's not supposed to feel like a revelation — it's supposed to feel like recognition.

The more you honour the simple messages, the more natural intuition becomes.

🌿 5. Stop Arguing With Your Inner Yes

You know those moments when you feel a strong yes — and then immediately talk yourself out of it?

That's where intuitive confidence erodes.

Every time you override your inner yes or inner no, you teach yourself that your truth isn't trustworthy.

But every time you honour it — even when it feels small, even when it feels inconvenient — you build a deeper sense of internal loyalty.

Confidence is the result of refusing to betray your own clarity.

6. Don't Expect Intuition to Remove All Fear

A powerful truth:

Intuition can feel right and still feel scary.

People assume that if something is intuitive, it will feel effortless, fearless, smooth.

But intuition often leads you into chapters you've never lived before.

And newness can feel uncomfortable.

Confidence grows when you stop waiting for fear to disappear and start choosing what feels aligned even with trembling hands.

🌿 7. Follow the Energy, Not the Logic

Intuition doesn't always make sense.

But it always makes movement.

- Follow what feels energizing.

- Follow what feels alive.

- Follow what feels like truth in your body, even if you can't explain it yet.

Confidence grows when you let your energy — not your old patterns — lead the way.

8. Return to Your Body Again and Again

Your mind doubts.

Your intuition doesn't.

When in doubt:

- place a hand on your chest

- breathe slowly

- ask, "What feels true right now?"

- notice the first sensation

The body doesn't lie.

It just asks you to listen more often.

Intuitive confidence expands every time you return to your body for answers your mind can't give.

9. Celebrate Every Moment You Trusted Yourself

Confidence grows through acknowledgment.

Through celebration.

Through recognition.

Every time you trusted your intuition —

- even a little
- even imperfectly
- even when scared
- even when uncertain

— your capacity for inner trust expanded.

Celebrate these moments.

- Name them.

- Honor them.

They are evidence of a relationship you're rebuilding with yourself.

🌿 Intuitive Confidence Is Self-Loyalty

At its core, intuitive confidence means:

- "I choose myself."

- "I trust my inner knowing."

- "I move with my truth."

- "I listen to the voice within me over the noise outside me."

It's a quiet kind of empowerment — not loud, not forceful — but steady, grounded, unmistakable.

This chapter is your reminder that intuitive confidence isn't built in a day.

It's built in moments.

Small, soft, consistent moments where you choose to believe yourself just a little more than you did yesterday.

When Intuition Leads You Somewhere Unexpected

Intuition doesn't always take you where you planned to go.

It takes you where you're meant to grow.

Sometimes your intuition leads you down a path that makes no logical sense.

- A direction you never imagined.

- A choice you didn't expect.

- A chapter you didn't see coming.

And that's the thing about intuition:

- It doesn't follow your plans.

- It follows your alignment.

This chapter is about those moments — the ones that feel surprising, disruptive, inconvenient, or strange — but ultimately transform your life in ways logic never could.

🌿 Intuition Isn't Predictable — It's Precise

Intuition won't always give you the full map.
It just gives you the next step.

Sometimes that step leads to:

- A person you weren't expecting.

- An opportunity you hadn't considered.

- A direction you'd never thought of.

or a version of yourself you didn't know you were ready to become.

It may not look like clarity at first, but it is clarity — just not the kind the mind understands.

🌿 1. The Detour That Isn't a Detour

Intuition often leads you off the path you planned because the path you planned is too small for you now.

What feels like a detour is usually alignment redirecting you.

Every time your intuition says:

- "Not that way."
- "Slow down."
- "Turn here."
- "Pause."
- "Wait."
- "This instead."

…it's not sabotaging you.

It's rearranging your life to match what you're becoming.

🌿 2. The Calling That Makes No Sense (Yet)

Some intuitions feel strange in the moment:

- Why am I drawn to this place?
- Why does this person feel significant?
- Why am I suddenly done with something I loved?
- Why does this feel important even though I don't know why?

These moments aren't accidents.
They're invitations.

Intuition sees what your mind can't:

- the connections ahead,

- the growth waiting for you,

- the alignment forming beneath the surface.

You're not meant to understand it immediately.

You're meant to follow it gently.

🌿 3. The Ending That Comes Suddenly

Sometimes intuition ends something before you're "ready":

- a job
- a friendship
- a dream
- a cycle
- a storyline

Intuition doesn't wait for the mind's permission.

When something is no longer aligned, intuition withdraws your energy from it.

You feel the shift long before you can explain it.

This isn't loss — it's truth making space.

🌿 4. The Impulse That Changes Everything

There are moments when intuition shows up as a spark:

- a sudden yes
- a sudden no
- a desire to move
- a desire to speak
- a desire to reach out
- a desire to walk away

These impulses aren't randomness.

They're alignment in motion.

One intuitive impulse can redirect the entire trajectory of your life in the gentlest way.

🌿 5. The Path That Feels Uncertain But Right

Intuition will often lead you into the unknown — not because you're lost, but because you're evolving.

The unknown feels uncomfortable, but intuition isn't trying to intimidate you.

It's trying to expand you.

If something feels:

- unfamiliar
- new
- strange
- unexpected
- but quietly right

— that's intuition leading you somewhere your old self couldn't go but your new self is ready for.

6. The Answer That Arrives Before the Explanation

One of the most powerful signs of intuition:

You know what to do long before you know why.

The "why" comes later — after the movement, after the growth, after the unfolding.

You don't wait for understanding to act.
Understanding waits for you to act.

The explanation always catches up to the intuition that came first.

🌿 7. Trusting the Unexpected

When intuition leads you somewhere unexpected:

- Trust the nudge.

- Trust the pull.

- Trust the quiet yes in your chest.

- Trust the door that opens easily.

- Trust the door that closes firmly.

- Trust the shift in your energy.

Trust the part of you that feels calm even in uncertainty.

Intuition never leads you to chaos — it leads you to alignment.

The unexpected is often your next chapter arriving early.

🌿 The Unexpected Path Is the True Path

You are not meant to walk a life that fits the old version of you.

Your intuition guides you toward the life that fits the real you.

Even when it surprises you.
Especially when it surprises you.

The unexpected path is the one that carries your expansion, your healing, your inner truth, your becoming.

This chapter is your reminder:

Intuition doesn't take you where you planned — it takes you where you belong.

Integrating Intuition Into Daily Life

Intuition isn't meant to exist only in big decisions or spiritual moments or quiet mornings.

It's meant to live with you in the ordinary rhythm of your days.

- In the way you choose,

- the way you respond,

- the way you breathe,

- the way you move through the world.

Intuition becomes powerful not when you hear it occasionally — but when it becomes the way you live.

🌿 Intuition Thrives in the Everyday

You don't need rituals, routines, or retreats to stay connected to your inner knowing.

- You need presence.

- You need honesty.

- You need small, consistent moments where you check in with yourself before checking out the world.

Intuition anchors itself in the simplest things:

- a pause

- a breath

- a feeling

- a whisper

- a sensation

- a knowing

These become your daily navigation points — not dramatic, not mystical — just true.

🌱 1. Begin Your Day With Yourself

Before you open your phone or open your calendar or open your mind to the world...

Open your awareness inward.

Ask yourself:

- "What do I feel today?"

- "What do I need today?"

- "What energy am I carrying?"

- "What direction feels aligned?"

This takes less than a minute, but it reconnects you to your Centre before the world pulls you away from it.

🌿 2. Let Your Body Guide Small Choices

Throughout the day, ask:

- "Does this feel open or tight?"

- "Light or heavy?"

- "Calm or contracted?"

- "Aligned or off?"

Your body will tell you what your mind hasn't processed yet.

Intuition doesn't require analysis — it requires noticing.

🌿 3. Use Pauses as Your Daily Compass

A three-second pause can save you from acting out of fear, habit, or pressure.

Before replying, choosing, or committing:

- Pause.

- Breathe.

- Feel.

Let your inner truth rise before the world rushes in.

🌿 4. Honor the Subtle No

Small no's protect you from big misalignments.

- No to unnecessary conversations.

- No to draining obligations.

- No to the pressure to explain yourself.

- No to the old version of you people still expect.

Every "no" that honours your energy strengthens your intuitive boundary.

🌿 5. Follow the Micro-Yes

Some signs of alignment are tiny:

- a spark

- a warmth

- a pull

- a soft excitement

- a gentle curiosity

- a sense of ease

These micro-yeses are intuition's way of steering you gently toward what is meant for you.

They may seem small, but they lead to big clarity over time.

🌿 6. Let Life Meet You Halfway

Intuition doesn't operate alone.

It works with the unfolding of your life.

Your job is to listen.

Life's job is to respond.

Not everything will arrive when you want it to — but everything meant for you arrives when you are aligned with it.

"What is meant for you will never bypass you. Intuition doesn't just guide you toward what's yours — it helps you recognize it when it arrives."

7. Trust Delays, Redirections, and Closed Doors

Integrating intuition into daily life means you stop seeing obstacles as failures and start seeing them as guidance.

- If something isn't moving, you're not meant to push it.

- If something falls away, you're not meant to hold it.

- If something closes, you're being redirected.

Intuition is not only the pull forward — it's the gentle pull away from what isn't aligned anymore.

🌿 8. Create Micro-Moments of Connection

Intuition doesn't require hours.

It requires intention.

Try:
- two minutes of breathing
- a quiet sip of tea

- standing still before leaving the house

- checking your body before answering messages

- ending the day with silence instead of screens

These micro-moments become daily rituals of returning home to yourself.

9. Let Your Life Become a Dialogue, Not a Chase

Most people chase clarity.

But intuition doesn't respond to chasing.

It responds to listening.

- You don't need to force answers.

- You don't need to hunt for signs.

- You don't need to pressure yourself into knowing.

Just stay open, aware, present.

Clarity comes to those who create space for truth to land.

🌿 Intuition Becomes a Lifestyle, Not an Event

When intuition becomes part of your daily life:

- You stop abandoning yourself.

- You slow down naturally.

- You notice the subtle.

- You choose from alignment.

- You trust your timing.

- You feel guided instead of lost.

Your days become quieter, but more meaningful.

- Less chaotic, but more connected.

- Less reactive, but more intentional.

And life begins to feel like a conversation between your inner truth and what the universe is bringing to you.

Because it is.

When Intuition Conflicts With Other People's Expectations

Your intuition will often guide you in a direction other people don't understand.

Not because they're unkind.
Not because they're against you.

But because your inner truth is designed for you, not for them.

People expect you to choose the paths that make sense to their minds, match their beliefs, and align with their comfort.

But intuition doesn't follow approval.
It follows authenticity.

This chapter is for the moments when following your inner guidance means disappointing someone, confusing someone, or stepping out of a role you were once praised for.

🌿 Intuition Is Personal — Expectations Are Collective

Intuition comes from your soul.

Expectations come from society, family, culture, and conditioning.

Intuition says:
"This feels right for me."

Expectations say:
"This is what people like you should do."

One liberates.

The other limits.

Your intuition serves your expansion — not your image.

🌿 1. People Expect You to Stay the Version of You They Knew

When you grow, it disrupts the roles you used to play.

- The quiet one.
- The people-pleaser.
- The helper.
- The dependable one.
- The strong one.
- The predictable one.

Your intuition will ask you to evolve beyond these roles.

But others may prefer the old version of you because it was comfortable for them.

You're not here to stay small just so others don't have to adjust.

🌿 2. Your Inner Yes May Look Like a No to Others

Sometimes intuition guides you toward:

- what others don't think is realistic
- what doesn't match their blueprint
- what threatens their comfort zone
- what breaks an unspoken rule
- what they never expected from you

But you aren't here to live a life designed by someone else's fears.

Your yes doesn't need universal agreement to be valid.

🌿 3. **Intuition Asks You to Choose Alignment

Even When Others Want Explanation**

When you follow intuition, people may ask:

- "Why would you do that?"
- "What if it doesn't work?"
- "Are you sure?"
- "What will people think?"
- "Why not just stay where you are?"

They're asking for logic to make sense of your inner knowing.

But intuition doesn't speak in justification.

It speaks in truth.

You don't owe anyone a presentation, a breakdown, or a logical pitch for what feels right in your soul.

🌿 4. When You Change Direction, People Feel Their Own Fears

When your intuition calls you somewhere new:

- someone may feel abandoned
- someone may feel threatened
- someone may feel insecure
- someone may feel left behind
- someone may feel exposed
- someone may feel uncomfortable

Your evolution mirrors their stagnation.

Your courage reflects their fear.

Your movement highlights their standstill.

Their reaction says everything about their inner world, and nothing about the truth of your path.

🌿 5. Disappointing Someone Is Not the Same as Doing Something Wrong

Read that again.

You are not responsible for managing other people's discomfort with your growth.

You are allowed to:

- choose again

- walk away

- change your mind

- outgrow old versions of yourself

- follow a path no one expects

- make choices that only make sense to you

Other people's expectations are not your obligations.

🌿 6. Intuition Will Sometimes Require Silence

You don't always need to defend your choices.

Some intuitions are meant to be protected until they take form.

- Sometimes silence is sacred.

- Sometimes privacy is power.

- Sometimes explanation dilutes truth.

When people question you, listen inward first.

Your intuition doesn't need a committee.

🌿 7. Your Life Is Not a Group Project

- You don't need consensus to live in alignment.

- You don't need agreement to follow your truth.

- You don't need approval to honour your knowing.

Every time you choose yourself over expectation, your intuitive strength grows.

🌿 When You Choose Intuition Over Expectation...

You step into your real life — not the life others scripted for you.

- You step out of old stories.
- Out of inherited patterns.
- Out of outdated identities.
- Out of roles that never fit.

And you step into:

- Clarity
- Freedom
- self-trust

- inner alignment

- quiet truth

- authentic direction

You become someone who honours their soul even when the world doesn't understand.

And that is where your life begins to feel like it finally belongs to you.

🌿 This Chapter's Truth

When you follow your intuition, you won't always be understood.

But you will always be aligned.

And in the end, alignment is what creates a life that feels deeply, unmistakably yours.

Becoming the Version of You Who Trusts Yourself Fully

There comes a moment on every intuitive path when you stop trying to "find" intuition and start becoming someone who naturally listens to their inner truth.

This chapter is that moment.

Becoming the version of you who trusts yourself fully is not about becoming fearless, perfect, or certain.

It's about becoming deeply loyal to your inner wisdom — even when it's quiet, even when it's inconvenient, even when it changes your life.

Self-trust isn't a skill.

- It's an identity.

- A way of being.

- A relationship with yourself

that cannot be shaken by doubt or noise.

You're not just learning intuition.

You're becoming someone who lives from it.

🌿 The Shift Happens Internally First

Before your actions change, your relationship with yourself does.

You begin to:

- take your own feelings seriously

- honour your internal signals

- stop abandoning yourself

- stop second-guessing every truth you feel

- stop searching outside for answers you already have

Self-trust grows quietly — one inner yes at a time.

🌿 1. You Stop Asking for Permission

You no longer wait for someone to validate:

- your desires

- your boundaries

- your instincts

- your choices

- your pace

- your path

You move because you feel the truth, not because someone else approves of it.

When you trust yourself, permission becomes internal — not outsourced.

🌿 2. You Listen to the Whisper Before the World Gets Loud

Most people hear intuition last.

But when you trust yourself fully, you learn to hear it first.

- Before fear.
- Before opinions.

- Before logic.
- Before pressure.
- Before expectation.

You don't have to force this — you simply become someone who naturally checks inward before checking outward.

🌿 3. You Know When Something Isn't Right, Even Without Evidence

Self-trust sharpens your sensitivity.

You don't need proof to honour:

- the discomfort
- the subtle shift
- the energetic no
- the closing in your body

- the quiet misalignment

You trust the initial feeling before your mind tries to override it.

- Your intuition becomes enough.

- Your body becomes enough.

- Your inner knowing becomes enough.

🌿 4. You Don't Betray Yourself to Keep the Peace

The old you may have:

- said yes when you meant no
- stayed quiet when you felt truth
- shrunk to avoid attention
- stayed to avoid hurting someone
- ignored red flags to be liked

- abandoned yourself for approval

But the you who trusts yourself fully understands that peace without self-honouring isn't peace — it's self-erasure.

You choose inner truth over external comfort.

🌿 5. You Stop Explaining Your Intuition to People Who Don't Feel It

You no longer translate your inner knowing into logical narratives just to be understood.

Some truths are not meant to be explained — only lived.

You trust your instincts without needing a panel of opinions to back them up.

🌿 6. You Let Your Timing Be Your Timing

The version of you who trusts yourself fully knows this:

- You are not late.

- You are not behind.

- You are not missing your moment.

You move when your soul says move, and you pause when your soul says pause.

And you trust it — even when it doesn't match the timeline of anyone around you.

🌿 7. You Accept That Growth Will Sometimes Feel Lonely

Becoming the real you often means leaving behind:

- old identities

- old habits

- old versions of you

- old relationships

- old ways of being safe

Self-trust sometimes creates space before it creates connection.

But the loneliness isn't emptiness — it's clearing.

- Clearing for people who match your truth.

- Clearing for opportunities aligned with your soul.

- Clearing for the life your intuition has been leading you toward.

🌿 8. You Trust Yourself Even When You're Afraid

Self-trust doesn't erase fear — it holds fear with compassion.

You don't wait for fear to disappear.

- You move with it.

- Beside it.

- Through it.

You understand that courage is not the absence of fear — it's the decision to trust yourself more than the fear.

🌿 Becoming the You Who Knows

You become someone who:

- knows when something is right

- knows when something is wrong

- knows when to stay

- knows when to leave

- knows when to speak

- knows when to silence

- knows what your body is saying

- knows what your heart is guiding

- knows when your soul says "this way"

This isn't arrogance.

This is self-alignment.

🌿 The Version of You Who Trusts Yourself Fully Already Exists

You're not becoming someone new.

You're returning to someone ancient within you.

- The you who knows.

- The you who feels.

- The you who recognizes truth instantly.

- The you who doesn't abandon themselves.

- The you who chooses alignment over approval.

- The you who listens inward first.

This chapter is your reminder:

Self-trust is not an achievement.

It's a homecoming.

Signs You're Living From Intuition

There's a quiet shift that happens when intuition becomes your normal way of living.

- It's not dramatic.
- It's not loud.
- It's not sudden.

It's subtle at first — like a soft internal alignment that grows stronger day by day until one morning you realize:

"I don't abandon myself anymore."

Living from intuition feels different.

- Your choices feel different.

- Your energy feels different.
- Your relationships feel different.

Your entire life begins to breathe differently.

This chapter is about recognizing those signs — the markers of inner transformation that show you're no longer navigating from fear or habit, but from truth.

🌿 1. You Feel Calm Even When You Don't Have All the Answers

Before, uncertainty felt threatening.
Now, uncertainty feels spacious.

You trust that clarity will come when it's time.

- You don't force decisions.
- You don't panic for answers.

- You don't pressure yourself to "figure it out."

You simply allow the next step to reveal itself the way intuition always does — naturally and in perfect timing.

🌿 2. You No Longer Need as Much External Validation

You used to look to others for direction:

- "Is this a good idea?"
- "Does this make sense?"
- "What would you do?"
- "Do you think this is right?"

But now you realize those were questions born from self-doubt — not truth.

Living from intuition means you trust your own sense of alignment more than the world's opinions. Approval is no longer your compass.

Your inner knowing is.

🌿 3. You Feel It in Your Body When Something Is Off

Your body speaks louder now.

You sense misalignment immediately:

- the tightening in your chest
- the sudden heaviness
- the shrinking sensation
- the subtle pull away
- the shift in energy

You don't ignore these signals anymore.

You respond to them.

Your body has become your guide, and you trust its wisdom.

🌿 4. You Choose What Feels Right, Not What Looks Right

You no longer make choices based on appearances, expectations, or logic alone.

You choose based on:

- resonance

- alignment

- peace

- truth

- inner clarity

Even when the choice surprises others.

Even when it surprises you.

You don't chase the impressive path — you choose the honest one.

🌿 5. You Notice Flow Instead of Forcing

- You stop pushing so hard.

- You stop trying to control everything.

- You stop running on urgency.

- You let life meet you halfway.

You trust:

- the delays

- the pauses

- the detours

- the redirections

- the ease

Because you've learned that what is meant for you comes with a feeling of openness — not resistance.

🌿 6. You're More Sensitive to Energy — in People, Places, and Choices

Intuition sharpens your perception.

You can feel:

- who feels nourishing

- who feels draining

- what environments support you

- what situations constrict you

- where your energy expands

- where it collapses

You don't overanalyse anymore.

You trust your energetic experience as real and valid information.

🌱 7. You Set Boundaries Without Apology

Living from intuition strengthens your self-respect.

- You say no without guilt.

- You leave when something isn't aligned.

- You stop overexplaining.

- You protect your peace.

- You choose environments that match your truth.

These aren't reactions — they're expressions of self-trust.

🌿 8. You Stop Betraying Yourself for Acceptance or Approval

- You don't pretend.

- You don't shrink.

- You don't shape-shift to fit.

- You don't override your feelings.

- You don't silence your truth to keep others comfortable.

You realize that losing yourself is too high a price to pay for being liked.

🌿 9. Your Life Begins to Feel More Like You

This is one of the clearest signs.

- You wake up feeling aligned.

- Your days feel more spacious.

- Your choices feel congruent.

- Your interactions feel genuine.

- Your relationships feel more balanced.

- Your direction feels true.

Your life stops feeling like something you're managing and starts feeling like something you're inhabiting.

🌿 10. Synchronicities Happen More Often

When you're in alignment, life responds.

You notice:

- the right people arriving at the right time

- doors opening effortlessly

- opportunities matching your energy

- signs appearing that confirm your direction
moments of perfect timing

This isn't magic — it's resonance.

When you live from intuition, your outer world aligns with your inner world.

🌿 11. You Trust Yourself Even When the Path Is Unfamiliar

The greatest sign of intuitive living:

You trust your steps even when you don't know the destination.

- You don't need a full map.

- You don't need guarantees.

- You don't need certainty.

You walk with inner confidence because you know:

What is meant for you will not bypass you.

And what is not meant for you will fall away gently.

🌿 Living From Intuition Feels Like Coming Home

Not to a place — but to yourself.

- You recognize your own signals.

- You honour your own pace.

- You follow your own truth.

- You feel guided instead of lost.

Supported instead of stressed.

Aligned instead of conflicted.

This chapter is your reflection point:

you are no longer someone searching for intuition.

You are someone living from it.

The Quiet Revolution Within You

There comes a moment on every inner journey when something soft but undeniable awakens inside you.

Not a spark — a shift.

Not a surge — a remembering.

A quiet revolution.

The kind that doesn't announce itself, but rewrites you from the inside out.

This book has been guiding you back to a truth you've always carried:

- You are not lost.
- You are not disconnected.
- You are not separate from your own wisdom.

You have simply been living drowned in noise loud enough to make you forget how powerful your inner knowing truly is.

But now…

you remember.

🌿 The Revolution Begins When You Choose Yourself

- Not loudly.
- Not dramatically.
- Not with grand declarations.

But with small, sacred choices:

- a breath before reacting

- a pause before deciding

- a moment of honesty with yourself

- a boundary quietly honoured, a truth you don't abandon

- a feeling you no longer override

This is how intuition takes root.

This is how self-trust rebuilds.

This is how you come home to yourself.

🌿 You Have Become Someone Who Listens

- You've learned the language of your body.

- You've learned the difference between intuition and fear.

- You've learned how to create space in a world that constantly pulls you away from yourself.

And somewhere along the way, without even realizing it...

you became someone who hears yourself again.

- Someone who recognizes the whisper.

- Someone who trusts the first truth.

- Someone who follows the resonance.

- Someone who honours alignment over expectation.

This is the revolution — the return of your inner authority.

🌿 The Quiet Strength You Carry Now

Is Not the Strength You Had Before...

- It's deeper.

- More rooted.

- More ancient.

It does not come from proving, performing, hustling, or pleasing.

It comes from listening — and responding to what you hear.

- Your strength now is intuitive.

- It moves from the inside out.

- It is guided, not forced.

- Aligned, not frantic.

- True, not reactive.

🌱 You Are No Longer Led by Fear

Fear may still speak — that is human.

But it no longer leads.

Your intuition has taken its place as the quiet leader of your life.

- You feel your truth faster.

- You honour your energy sooner.

- You trust your knowing more easily.

- You choose alignment over habit without apology.

You have shifted the axis you live from.

🌿 An Inner Revolution Always Changes the Outer World

As your alignment deepens, your life will begin to rearrange to match the person you've become.

- People will shift.

- Paths will open.

- Old cycles will fall away.

- New opportunities will rise.

- Relationships will evolve.

- Your environment will respond to the clarity you now carry.

You don't have to chase anything — your life will meet you where your intuition stands.

🌿 You Are Becoming Who You Were Always Meant to Be

- Not the version shaped by fear.
- Not the version shaped by expectations.
- Not the version shaped by survival.

But the version shaped by truth.

- By resonance.

- By inner wisdom.

- By spiritual alignment.

This is your becoming.

A return to the soul-level clarity that was never lost — only buried.

🌿 The Quiet Revolution Will Continue

This final chapter is not an ending.

It's a threshold.

- You will keep evolving.

- You will keep listening.

- You will keep rising

into deeper layers of your intuition.

And every time you hear that gentle knowing within you, you'll remember:

You started a revolution the moment you chose to trust yourself.

🌿 And Now… the Journey Is Yours

- Take what resonates.

- Leave what no longer serves.

- Walk the path your intuition lights — step by quiet, courageous step.

Because the truth is simple and powerful:

You were never meant to live disconnected from your own knowing.

You were meant to live guided.

- Aligned.

- Awake.

- Whole.

And now that you've returned to the deepest part of yourself…

the world will never look the same again.

This is your quiet revolution.

And it has only just begun.

Intuition Journaling Spread — Your Inner Voice on Paper

Use this space to explore the truth that rises when you slow down enough to hear it.

There are no right answers — only honest ones.

 1. The Clearest Yes in My Life Right Now

What in your life currently feels like a full-body yes?

- Where do you feel it?
- What does it open in you?

Write freely:

What is calling you forward right now?

🌱 2. The Quiet No I've Been Avoiding

- What have you been holding onto that no longer feels aligned?

- Where does your body resist?

Write gently:

What truth have you been whispering to yourself but not yet honouring?

🌱 3. A Moment I Ignored My Intuition — and What It Taught Me

Think of a time you overrode your knowing.

- What did you feel in the moment?

- What pulled you away from that feeling?

- What did you learn about yourself?

- What would you choose differently now?

🌿 4. A Moment I Followed My Intuition — and It Changed Something

Recall a time your inner knowing guided you well.

- What was the sign?

- How did you recognize it?

- What unfolded because of it?

Write with pride:

How did trusting yourself shift your path?

🌿 5. Where I Still Don't Trust Myself Fully

This is not weakness — it's awareness.

- What areas of life still trigger doubt?
- Where do you silence yourself?
- Where does fear speak louder than truth?

What would trusting yourself here look like?

🌿 6. What My Body Wants Me to Know Today

Place your hand on your chest or stomach.

Breathe.

Listen inward.

Then write:

- What is my body asking for right now?

- What sensation is speaking?

- What truth lies beneath it?

🌿 7. My Relationship With My Intuition Is Becoming...

Finish this sentence as many times as you need:

"My relationship with my intuition is becoming..."

- Softer

- Clearer

- Stronger

- Easier

- more familiar

- more sacred

- more natural

Let the words unfold.

🌱 8. A Promise I Want to Make to Myself

Think of one act of self-loyalty you want to commit to.

- A boundary.

- A yes.

- A no.

- A slowing down.

- A pause.

- A truth you won't abandon again.

Write it as a vow:

"I promise to…"

🌿 9. The Intuitive Version of Me

Describe the version of yourself who:

- moves from clarity
- listens inward first
- trusts their instincts
- honours their energy
- follows resonance
- sets boundaries with grace

- chooses alignment over expectation

Who is this version of you?

How do they move through the world?

What choices do they make?

What does their life feel like?

Write as if you're introducing them to yourself.

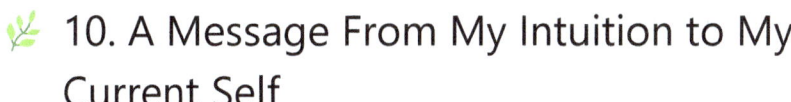 10. A Message From My Intuition to My Current Self

Close your eyes.

Breathe.

Ask inward:

What do you want me to know?

Then let the words spill onto the page...

- Don't edit.

- Don't analyse.

Just receive.

🌿 Closing Reflection

What was the most revealing part of this journaling spread — and why?

This page is your first step toward a deeper intuitive unfolding.

Intuition Assessment Quiz — How Closely Are You Living From Inner Knowing?

This is not a score.

It's a reflection — a soft doorway into self-awareness.

Answer instinctively.
Trust the first response that rises.

For each statement, choose:
Often • Sometimes • Rarely

🌿 1. I can sense when something feels "off" even if I can't explain why.

Often / Sometimes / Rarely

🌿 2. I notice shifts in my body —
openness, tightness, heaviness, ease —
and consider them meaningful.

Often / Sometimes / Rarely

🌿 3. I pause before reacting or deciding,
giving space for clarity to rise.

Often / Sometimes / Rarely

🌿 4. I can tell the difference between my
intuition and my fear.

Often / Sometimes / Rarely

🌿 5. I trust my first instinct more than external opinions.

Often / Sometimes / Rarely

🌿 6. I no longer override my inner "no" to please others or keep the peace.

Often / Sometimes / Rarely

🌿 7. I feel drawn toward certain people, choices, or paths without needing to justify it.

Often / Sometimes / Rarely

🌿 8. When something doesn't feel right, I honour the feeling instead of talking myself out of it.

Often / Sometimes / Rarely

🌿 9. I feel calm in uncertainty because I trust that clarity will come.

Often / Sometimes / Rarely

🌿 10. I make decisions based on alignment, not pressure or expectation.

Often / Sometimes / Rarely

⭐ Your Intuitive Profile

If you answered "Often" to most statements:

- You're living from intuitive alignment.

- Your inner voice is no longer a whisper — it's become your way of moving through life.

- Keep honouring it.

- Keep trusting it.

You're in the flow.

*****

If you answered a mix of "Often" and "Sometimes":

- You are reconnecting beautifully.

- You're learning to hear yourself again, softening old patterns, and strengthening new ones.

Your intuition is strengthening each time you pause, listen, and choose truth over noise.

*****

If you answered mostly "Sometimes" and "Rarely":

- You are in the remembering stage — the doorway.

- This book found you at the perfect time.

- Your intuition is still present, still alive, still waiting gently.

The more space you create, the more loudly it will rise.

*****

⭐ A Closing Reflection

What question in this quiz felt the strongest to you — and why?

Your answer to that one question reveals where your next level of intuitive growth begins.

The Light You Carry Forward

When you close this book, nothing truly ends.

You don't go back to who you were before these pages found you.

You don't return to the noise that once drowned your inner truth.

You don't forget the wisdom your body has relearned to speak.

Something inside you has shifted — quietly, but irrevocably.

You've reclaimed a connection that was always yours, even in the seasons you felt furthest from it.

This book didn't give you intuition.
It reminded you of it.

It showed you the doorway inward and the light waiting behind it.

A light that has always belonged to you.

🌿 **You will still have noisy days.

You will still doubt.
You will still forget.**

This is part of being human.

- But now you recognize the difference.

- Now you know how to return.

- Now you understand how to find your way back to the quiet truth inside you.

Even when you wander, you won't wander far.

Even when you drift, you won't drift long.

Intuition has become your compass again — a steady, familiar guide that lives within you no matter what the world asks of you.

🌿 The journey continues, but differently now

- Not from searching, but from remembering.
- Not from urgency, but from presence.
- Not from fear, but from alignment.

You will carry this knowing into your conversations, your relationships, your choices, your inner world.

- It will shape the way you speak to yourself.

- It will soften the way you move through your days.

- It will illuminate the places you once walked blindly.

And you'll notice moments — small but profound — where you choose differently because you feel differently.

- This is growth.

- This is inner evolution.

- This is the quiet revolution finding its way into your everyday life.

🌱 If you remember only one thing, let it be this:

- Your intuition has never left you.
- It has never dimmed.
- It has never stopped calling you home.
- You don't need to earn it.

- You don't need to perfect it.
- You don't need to chase it.

You only need to create space for the truth you already carry to rise again.

🌿 So take a breath… and take this with you:

- You are guided.

- You are supported.

- You are aligned.

- You are connected to wisdom far deeper than your thoughts.

And every time you pause, every time you listen inward, every time you trust that quiet knowing…

you step further into the life that was always meant for you.

Because what is meant for you will never bypass you.

- Not when you're living from truth.

- Not when you're listening inward.

- Not when you're walking in alignment with the deepest part of yourself.

This is not the end.

It's the beginning of you meeting your life with open eyes, open energy, and an open soul.

Your next chapter is unfolding already.

And you're ready for it.

★

www.ingramcontent.com/pod-product-compliance
Lightning Source LLC
Chambersburg PA
CBHW052030070526
44584CB00016B/1978